Organ Pipe

Gregory McNamee, SERIES EDITOR

Organ Pipe
Life on the Edge

TEXT BY Carol Ann Bassett

PHOTOGRAPHS BY Michael Hyatt

The University of Arizona Press   Tucson

The University of Arizona Press
Text © 2004 Carol Ann Bassett
Photographs © 2004 Michael Hyatt

♾ This book is printed on acid-free, archival-quality paper.

Manufactured in the United States of America

09 08 07 06 05 04   6 5 4 3 2 1

Library of Congress Cataloging-in-Publication Data appear on the last
printed page of this book.

Frontispiece: Organ pipe cactus with cristate formations.

contents

photographs

PHOTOGRAPHS

X

preface

I first came to Organ Pipe Cactus National Monument in the spring of 1988. It was a remote and rugged wilderness in the Sonoran Desert—hot, prickly, and easy to get lost in. Yet, there was something that kept drawing me back: the wide-open spaces, the crystalline light, the surprising diversity of desert life. I wanted to know how this landscape had evolved from a shallow sea, to a realm where juniper, piñon, and oak trees once flourished, to a desert that received less than ten inches of rainfall a year. Everything here struggled to survive in the blazing Arizona sun, yet for much of the year the land was vibrant and green, unlike the other North American deserts I had visited.

In spring, scarlet blossoms dangled from spindly ocotillos. Wild-flowers turned the desert into a tapestry of yellow, purple, and white. Cactus bloomed everywhere: prickly pear, barrel, cholla, organ pipe, senita, and saguaro. It seemed less like a desert than a vast green oasis, a place that in many ways felt like another world.

When Gregory McNamee, editor of the Desert Places series, invited me to write a book about Organ Pipe, I was delighted to return to the monument. I had never met Michael Hyatt, the book's photographer, but a friend and I hooked up with him in Organ Pipe in August—the hottest time of the year unless it rains. Michael was a quiet man, and I appreciated his patience while making a photograph—his eye for light, texture, and com-position, and his willingness to plod through the desert even though it was 104 degrees. I watched him at work, document-ing a collared lizard perched on a rock, the weird rock forma-tions in the Ajo Mountains, and the ancient campsites of those who had once lived there.

My own intention was to write a sensitive book about the natural and cultural history of the monument, to capture the beauty and mystery of the desert's natural rhythms so that oth-ers might also appreciate them. I wanted to share my deepest feelings about Organ Pipe and why it has always been for me a place of solitude and refuge. I also wanted to show how this fragile wilderness has changed in the last few years and why the monument must be protected now more than ever.

A note of clarification on the use of the terms *park* and *monu-ment*. I have used them interchangeably throughout the narrative for simplicity's sake. The difference between the two is that national parks are established by Congress to inspire, educate, and provide recreation. National monuments are created, often by presidential proclamation, to preserve prehistoric, cultural, and natural resources.

I owe many people thanks for helping me with this book. I am especially grateful to Greg McNamee, whose own writing I have long admired. His encouragement and good cheer were always inspiring. Thanks, too, to acquiring editor Patti Hartmann, especially for help with the book's title. This book could not have been possible without the help of the good people at Organ Pipe Cactus National Monument: superintendent Bill Wellman, plant ecologist Sue Rutman, wildlife biologist Tim Tibbitts, and chief ranger Fred Patton. Finally, I'd like to thank my friend John Russial for accompanying me on my latest visit to Organ Pipe, and for reading the manuscript. As always, his insights and suggestions were very thoughtful.

Photographer Michael Hyatt wishes to thank Organ Pipe Cactus National Monument biological technician Ami Pate for her assistance.

Organ Pipe

the shape of the land

Few places have aroused in me what could be called a defining moment—a brush so wide with life that I can never again be the same. Years ago I found such a place—a remote desert oasis in southern Arizona full of ebony mountains, golden poppies, and stately saguaros. Organ Pipe Cactus National Monument was a fragile terrain where I learned to pay attention to the details. The slower my eye moved, the more it took in: the tracks of a sidewinder in the sand, the tiny eggs of a canyon wren, the flash of a vermilion flycatcher against the azure sky. I loved April when the wind sailed down through the soft bark of the blue palo verde trees, sending golden blossoms out over the land like so many butterflies. But what moved me most was the rain in August as it coursed down normally dry arroyos, gouging out cactus, shrubs, and even the nests of wrens. There were times, too, when the rain drifted down through the hot desert sky like a glistening net, evaporating before ever touching the earth. It was a magical realm where everything struggled to hang on—to escape the threat of heat and talon and fang—a place where I could observe the biggest mystery of all: impermanence. It was also a sanctuary where I could think and dream and write—a place where I could learn to trust my instincts and find an opening for my heart. As Anaïs Nin is said to have written, "There came a time when the risk to remain tight in the bud was more painful than the risk it took to blossom."

In the spring I load my car with camping gear and head out for the monument about three hours southwest of my home in Tucson. I pass through a few scattered villages of the Tohono O'odham Nation, where horses graze in the shadows of Baboquivari Peak, and turn south on the highway leading to Mexico. This region is one of the most forbidding places on the North American continent. Here, in the dead of summer, the air temperature can reach 120 degrees; the ground can soar to 180, searing the soles of your shoes. When I arrive at the monument in mid-morning, it's already 92 degrees.

Across the valley to the west, the land opens like a gigantic fan. Heat waves rise from the earth like restless spirits, and in the scorching air the mountains undulate and melt into one another until they are no longer distinguishable. The sun creeps over the land, igniting the saguaros like torches. Everything is a kaleidoscope of green and tan and bronze, crossed by basins and peaks, all testifying to the dynamic forces at play here throughout the eons. How do deserts form? I wonder. How do plants and wildlife adapt in a land of so little rain? Why does the emptiness of the land turn us inward? These are questions I hope to answer as I explore the monument alone over the next six months.

At Alamo Canyon I strap on my backpack and hike into the Ajo Mountains. From here I can see Montezuma's Head, a lofty peak called I'itoi Mo'o in the O'odham language, or 'Oks Daha, "old woman sitting." When the trail forks, I follow the streambed north, scrambling over boulders and sashaying around cactus. It seems all the plants have thorns; it's their way of protecting themselves from nibbling passersby. I'm on constant guard for rattlesnakes, though I don't see or hear any along the trail. A few miles up the canyon, I find a rock ledge polished smooth by water and stop to look around. It's flat and it has a good view, so I set up my tent. This is the first time I've ever camped out alone, and I pray I will not be stung by a scorpion or break my leg in a fall. In the desert there's a fine line between courage and foolishness: You can get lost here. You can die and never be found.

Twilight. I sit on the ledge, watching the light change from amber to blue as darkness descends over the desert like a giant cloak. The first bats emerge from rock crevices and flutter on the warm desert air, and in the sapphire dome of the sky, the stars emerge like polished gems. That night I lie in my tent with

Montezuma's Head, Pitahaya Canyon.

a flashlight reading a delightful little book written by John C. Van Dyke called *The Desert*. Van Dyke was an art history professor at Rutgers University who in 1898 set out to explore the desert with his terrier, Cappy, strapped onto the back of his horse. Van Dyke suffered from asthma and depression, yet in his beautiful solitude he wrote one of the most passionate classics ever published about the desert. After reading only the first few pages, I sense that this man will set the tone for my wanderings. "There is something very restful about the horizontal line," he wrote. "Things that lie flat are at peace and the mind grows peaceful with them."

Dawn comes warm and bright. I lie on a flat rock watching the clouds parade above me. There's a stallion with mane as white as snow, a flock of sheep, an embryo curled inside a womb. There's a man with a beard and a Siamese cat, a big puffy fish and a girl with a hat. I imagine many things, but they do not last.

It's April and the saguaros have begun to bloom. Throughout the valley, white-winged doves emerge from the ivory blossoms with golden haloes of pollen. Clusters of organ pipe cactus rise from the ground with more than a dozen ribbed arms. Near the Estes Canyon–Bull Pasture trailhead I hike along the canyon floor, following a well-worn footpath. Webs spun overnight in the bushes cling to my thighs like silk, and a faint morning wind rustles my hair. When the trail forks I climb a steep, rugged path, stopping to catch my breath and to admire the wildflowers along the way: purple lupine and claret-colored penstemon whose tubular flowers attract hummingbirds. Soon I arrive at Bull Pasture—a broad plateau where ranchers once wintered their cattle in the protection of the rocks. I eat lunch here and gaze north across a series of ridgelines.

From up here, the Ajo Mountains look so tortured they could have come from a painting by Hiëronymus Bosch. Shattered by volcanic explosions, warped and thrust upward by faulting, blasted by wind, rain and sand, these mountains are the tallest and most rugged in the monument. For centuries, they were home to native hunters and gatherers who left behind stone hearths and sleeping circles, and who drank water from natural rock cisterns called *tinajas*. The Ajo Mountains were formed between 16 and 18 million years ago: layers of chestnut rhyolite, rosy breccia, and long golden bands of volcanic ash called tuff. At Bull Pasture a dozen cone-shaped figures jut sharply from the earth. They look like wizards' hats. A rock formation called the Sphinx stands nearby, and serrated ridges rise like the backbone of a stegosaurus. It's one of the most beautiful places I know—improbably so, given its weird appearance, but impossible to put out of my mind all the same.

Organ Pipe Cactus National Monument is a place of edges—an intersection of distinct environments that come together to create a wide diversity of life. Unlike the other three major North American deserts—the Chihuahuan, Mojave, and Great Basin—the Sonoran Desert is considered subtropical: low, hot, and relatively frost-free. The most biologically diverse desert on the continent, it's the only one that receives two rainy seasons a

Prehistoric sleeping circle, Ajo Mountains.

year—an average of nine inches in winter and summer. Shaped like a giant horseshoe, this 120,000-square-mile area covers southwestern Arizona, southeastern California, most of the Baja peninsula and its islands in the Gulf of California, and the western half of the state of Sonora, Mexico. It includes the Pinacate region southwest of the monument—a landscape of sand dunes, lava flows, and giant craters where in 1970 astronauts trained for the Apollo 14 mission to the moon. Organ Pipe lies in the north-central portion of the Sonoran Desert. The 516-square-mile monument was established in 1937 by President Franklin Delano Roosevelt to protect the area's historic landmarks and its unusual flora, especially the organ pipe cactus for which the monument was named.

This is a place of beauty and austerity—home to the night-blooming cereus, whose petals open on a single summer's eve then die with the morning sun; the bulbous gray elephant tree that "bleeds" a red sap if punctured; and the towering saguaro that can live to be two hundred years old. This is the realm of the eight-eyed wolf spider, the black and pink Gila monster, and the giant hairy tarantula. It's a whimsical place that could easily have come from the pages of Lewis Carroll. The saguaro is kin to the rose; the agave is a sister of the pineapple; the yucca is a kind of lily; and the mesquite is a giant mutant pea.

The organ pipe cactus itself was named by someone who thought it resembled the pipes of an old-fashioned organ. To me, it looks more like a prickly green octopus turned on its head. The plant comes from the subtropics of Mexico and reaches the northern limits of its range in and near the monument.

Its abundance here was one of the main reasons this diverse pocket of the Sonoran Desert was set aside as a national monument.

From the Ajo Mountains about four thousand feet above the desert floor, it's difficult to imagine that shallow seas once covered the land we now call Arizona. During the Paleozoic era, 570 million to 240 million years ago, the western United States lay quiet; North America had not yet broken away from the supercontinent, Pangaea, and drifted to its present place on the map. For 300 million years, tectonic plates shifted beneath the earth, allowing the western sea to advance and retreat over the shallow slope of the western United States perhaps a dozen times. With the sea came a flurry of primeval life: Marine lilies bobbed on the turquoise waves; Trilobites, brachiopods, sponges, and other invertebrates thrived in the warm, tropical waters. When the climate warmed during the Mesozoic era 230 million to 65 million years ago, the earth gave rise to dinosaurs, flying reptiles, birds, primitive mammals, flowering plants, and trees. Tropical rainforests and giant lakes covered much of the West, and palm trees fluttered in the breeze in what is now Alaska.

During the Cenozoic era, 65 million years ago to the present, the shallow seas finally drained away, leaving a geological legacy in stone: a storybook of fossils. When the dinosaurs disappeared, the age of mammals began, giving rise to mastodons, mammoths, ground sloths, giant beavers, dire wolves, and saber-toothed cats. The Rocky Mountains emerged in the West, and from their flanks sprang the headwaters of the two great western rivers—the Rio Grande and the Colorado. As the Sierra Nevada pushed upward to the west, the towering mountains blocked the eastward flow of moist Pacific air, giving birth to the North American deserts. The land dried out. Lava bubbled up through great faults in the earth's crust, solidifying into mountains. Broad alluvial valleys opened between the peaks, creating the Basin and Range topography of the American West.

During the last million years, great ice sheets formed in Canada and crept southward into the United States, not once but at least four times. The glaciers never reached the Organ Pipe area, but the region was much wetter and cooler. Ten thousand years ago, juniper, piñon, and oak flourished in the Ajo Mountains. Mammoths, giant sloths, and tapirs roamed the valleys below.

Strangely enough, it wasn't the giant mammals that provided clues to the region; it was the lowly pack rat. This small gray rodent hoards anything it can find: seeds, cactus joints, insects, small mammal bones, the teeth of bats, the scales of lizard, and even plastic cigarette lighters, as I would see on one of my hikes in the monument. The rodent stores these objects and later discards them in untidy middens—organic trash heaps cemented with fecal pellets and urine. By doing so, the pack rat has provided a revealing window on the past dating back more than fifty thousand years. Within these fossilized museums, paleoclimatologists have discovered the chips of a mammoth tooth from thirty thousand years ago, and potsherds and twine made by human hands twelve hundred years ago.

Pack rat den, Sonoyta Mountains.

Dozens of these prehistoric pack rat middens have been found in Organ Pipe, although no one knows exactly how many. The middens provide clues to ancient climates and life forms, and radiocarbon dating has shown when various species of plants and animals flourished during the last Ice Age. The dens have also revealed which plants retreated northward to cooler climates as the area became warmer, and they indicate almost precisely when the plants that are now so typical of the Sonoran Desert migrated up from the moist Mexican subtropics.

The saguaro first arrived in this region between nine and eleven thousand years ago when the Ice Age was waning. The organ pipe followed about four thousand years ago, when the great pyramids were being built in Egypt. These cacti would eventually dominate parts of the desert. They would also play a vital role in helping sustain the region's earliest humans, who arrived in the area about twelve thousand years ago—and some say much longer ago than that.

first people

One morning in May I drive down the dirt road through the Puerto Blanco Mountains. The saguaros are in full bloom, and the organ pipes have begun to blossom. Near the western lip of the mountains, I park my car and hike into the foothills, looking for a good place to camp. Ocotillos rise against an indigo sky, their thin red blossoms floating on the air like tropical birds. It takes me a while to find a spot that feels right. Finally, I come upon seven young saguaros that stand in a horseshoe formation overlooking the Valley of the Ajo. I dub my site "Seven Saguaro Camp" and use it as a base to go exploring. All around there are signs that others have been here before me: coyotes have left scat full of seeds, lizards have made patterns in the sand, and flickers have pecked holes into the saguaros. It's the perfect campsite, and I use the seven saguaros as a headboard for my desert bed.

Campfires aren't allowed in the park, so in the evening I make dinner on my small backpacking stove: fresh Gulf of California shrimp sautéed in garlic butter, with avocados, white cheese, salsa, and flour tortillas. The view from here is magnificent. To the east stand the jagged peaks of the Ajos; the smaller Cipriano Hills rise to the west. The Puerto Blanco Mountains extend south, and the Valley of the Ajo opens to the north. This broad plain once served as a trade route for the exchange of goods and ideas among ancient cultures, some argue as long as forty thousand years ago.

Much of the speculation about Organ Pipe's earliest inhabitants comes from the work of archaeologist Julian Hayden, a legendary desert rat who spent four decades doing fieldwork in the volcanic Sierra Pinacate region southwest of the monument. Hayden, whose findings remain controversial to this day, believed that the first people to set foot in this region were members of a hunter-gatherer culture called the Malpais, a Spanish word meaning "badland." The Malpais created crude chopper-scraper tools, small knives, and gouges out of heavy bivalve seashells from the nearby Gulf of California. Hayden based much of his theory on the radiocarbon dating of desert varnish, or organic patina, that had accumulated on the artifacts, though the methods used to date these items were later disputed. But Hayden, who believed his findings had fallen on the deaf ears of conventional archaeology, maintained his belief that the Malpais had lived in the region until about nineteen thousand years ago, when a great drought set in and pushed the culture out.

Most archaeologists believe that about eleven thousand years ago, a different culture entered the Organ Pipe area. These nomads were known as the San Dieguito people—Ice Age hunter-gatherers who collected fruit and seeds from the surrounding mountains and stalked game in the valleys below. Clues to their presence lie all over the monument.

One day in the Ajo Mountains I find an arrowhead made of shiny black obsidian. As I run my fingers over its serrated edges, I wonder what kind of beast it might have pierced, or whether the hunter missed, or whether it fell from his deerskin bag when he abandoned camp. I hold it up to the light to examine its perfect symmetry, then set it back on the ground where it has lain for perhaps thousands of years. There are other clues here as well: sleeping circles, trail shrines, rock cairns, ancient quarries, and tools fashioned from jasper, quartzite, and chert. The San Dieguito people, like those who followed, carved petroglyphs into the dark basalt stones of the desert, often to indicate where a trail forked or where water was present. In some parts of the desert, they scraped abstract etchings called geoglyphs into the desert floor.

On a warm spring night in the Pinacate region southwest of Organ Pipe, where these early cultures once lived, I sit with a friend on a huge basalt rock contemplating the vastness of space.

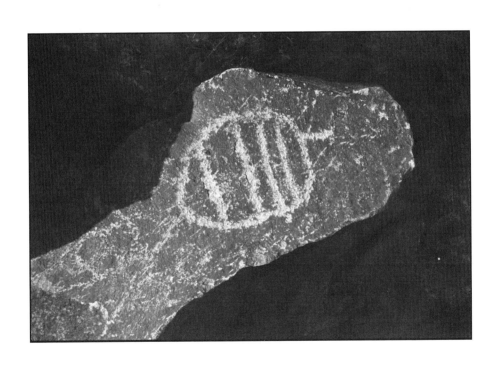

Petroglyph, Bates Mountains.

There, as usual, are Perseus, Cassiopeia, and the Pleiades. These are familiar constellations, ones I can easily see from my front yard in Tucson. What isn't familiar and what frightens us both out of our wits that night are the strange lights that suddenly appear northeast of the Pinacate sand dunes. They're arranged in a triangle and dazzlingly bright, and they move erratically over the desert as though trapped in a different dimension. Years later I write this poem:

Pinacate

Somewhere in the desert
between the smooth white dunes
and the blackened basalt
we watch the stars unfold one by one
until something unexpected and bright
appears to the east moving not straight
but upwards and down
then left to right
as though writing an equation
not of this world
yet late we gaze from our perch on stones
transfixed by what we see
not knowing what or when or where
yet certain no illusion plays before our eyes
then south above a crater
where spacemen trained
to drive a cart across the moon
it moves again

but slower and not so close
before vanishing
in the big black dome of the sky
and now nearly ten years later
I wonder still what happened that night
and what was lost and gained
and whether the flying lights
were ever meant for these human eyes.

The human story in this region is elusive at best. Had it not been for the discovery in the 1940s of nearby Ventana Cave, little would be known about the desert's early inhabitants. Until recently, there was little evidence to link prehistoric humans with the now-extinct mammals they had once hunted. Ventana Cave—a kind of primeval time capsule—shed new light on an old mystery. There, archaeologists—including Julian Hayden—uncovered the first stratified deposits of culture in the region. In the cave's lowest level, scientists found fossilized bones of tapirs, dire wolves, ground sloths, and bison dating back some 12,600 years. In the second-lowest level, dating back about 11,300 years, came the startling discovery of humans. Alongside the extinct Ice Age mammals they had hunted lay their artifacts: arrowheads, hammer stones, scrapers, and beautifully etched seashells. What was it like, I wonder, to live in this cave protected by sun and rain and wind, to gaze out and see herds of mammoth grazing on tall grasses? Why did these Ice Age mammals finally disappear?

At the end of the last Ice Age, another great drought set in.

It lasted at least four thousand years, drastically altering the landscape and making life unbearable. When a cooler climate returned, a culture called the Amargosa walked into the valley. The Amargosans, like those before them, fashioned chipped stone tools, and for the first time in the area created a sophisticated kind of projectile point. They made metates, manos, mortars, and pestles for grinding seeds into flour to make porridge, cakes, and bread.

In the millennia to follow, other cultures passed through the Valley of the Ajo on their way to the Gulf of California to collect seashells and salt. To get there they had to skirt the Pinacate lava flows, a sea of convoluted black rocks that are so sharp they can rip through the soles of your shoes. They also climbed tall shifting dunes leading down to the gulf, sinking in the peach-colored sand as they reached the crest lines, only to find more dunes up ahead.

Prehistoric farmers known as the Hohokam followed between fourteen hundred and eight hundred years ago. Organ Pipe lay on a path between their villages to the north and the gulf to the south, where they traveled to collect seashells for trade and personal adornment. They carved them into bracelets, armbands, and pendants with symbols of birds, frogs, and snakes, and etched designs into some of them with pitch and the fermented juice of saguaro fruit. The Hohokam established dozens of villages in the monument area, including one at Kuakatch Wash, where they dug a reservoir to reach permanent groundwater. Throughout their travels they relied on the few seeps and springs in the monument, especially those at

Quitobaquito Springs, a rare desert oasis in the southwest corner of the monument.

The Tohono O'odham—the "Desert People" who are most likely descendants of the Hohokam—came next. Men and boys trekked down to the sea to collect salt on a pilgrimage said to endow novices with visions and power. One salt route led to Mount Ajo and Quitobaquito Springs, then south to Pinacate Peak in northern Sonora where I'itoi—"Elder Brother" in O'odham oral history—landed after a great flood.

When the first Europeans arrived in 1540, they referred to the natives they encountered in the nearby sand dunes as Areneros, or "Sand People." These Hia Ced O'odham spoke—and their descendants still speak—a dialect of the Piman language common to other O'odham peoples in the region. They knew the Organ Pipe area well and were nicknamed for their ability to gather the plants, lizards, and mice that lived in the sand dunes. When enough rain fell, they farmed on a very small scale, raising corn, tepary beans, and squash. Their main staples, though, were protein-rich beans from mesquite, palo verde, and ironwood trees. In the centuries to follow, a small number of Hia Ced O'odham settled at Quitobaquito. The springs would later nourish the first explorers and missionaries, and thousands of prospectors who passed through the region looking for gold.

outsiders

I wake before dawn to the whimsical song of a canyon wren, whose descending scale resembles laughter: "HEE-HEE-HEE-HEE-hoo-hoo-hoo-hoo." A full moon still hangs on the western horizon like a bright amber globe. I make coffee, pack some raisins and an orange into my daypack, and drive down the primitive Puerto Blanco road straight into that shining orb toward Quitobaquito Springs. All the world looks blue: the organ pipes, the prickly pears, the copper-filled rocks that glint sapphire in the moonlight.

Quitobaquito is a true oasis in the dry and dusty monument, and when I arrive, a lone nighthawk swoops down and skims

Cottonwood tree at Quitobaquito Springs.

the surface of the pond, leaving a ring of concentric circles. Near water's edge a delicate blue dragonfly deposits eggs with the tip of her tail, and just beyond the reeds a Sonoyta mud turtle pokes its head through the water before disappearing in a shaft of bubbles. Flocks of ducks circle raucously to the south, and dozens of white-winged doves fly back and forth across the pond. Soon the sun climbs over the hills, casting a bright orange glow over the water. Two dark phainopeplas greet the day with eyes as red as rubies. A solitary vireo lands on the gnarly branch of a cottonwood tree. Yesterday I watched a great blue heron wade through these shallow waters feeding on insects and frogs. Now, a small black phoebe perches on a low-lying branch, catching one fly after another.

Quitobaquito lies about two hundred yards north of the Mexican border. The source of this tiny Eden is two natural springs, which are believed to originate in an ancient fault in the Quitobaquito Hills. William T. Hornaday, a field naturalist and taxidermist who stopped at the pond in 1907 on his way to the Pinacate volcanic fields, found the site "depressing" and later wrote in *Campfires on Desert and Lava:* "It is one of the spots in which I would not like to die, and would hate to live." A few years later, the Norwegian explorer Carl Lumholtz visited the pond and described it differently in his book *New Trails in Mexico:* "The tiny stream, fed by the springs, carries beautiful, limpid water amid banks white with mineral salts; the fresh green weeds at the bottom are also refreshing to behold."

Quitobaquito was one of the few reliable water sources in the region for the first explorers and missionaries, and for thousands of prospectors who passed through in the 1840s and 1850s seeking their fortunes in the California gold fields. Most often they followed a route called El Camino del Diablo, "the Devil's Highway." It began in the Mexican town of Caborca, meandering northwest of the Pinacate lava flows in El Gran Desierto, a region the writer and environmental activist Edward Abbey once described as "an iron-hard, iron-hued wilderness of craters, cones, congealed lava flows . . . the bleakest, flattest, hottest, grittiest, grimmest, dreariest, ugliest, most useless, most senseless desert of them all."

The Devil's Highway was one of the most perilous routes in the region, especially near Quitobaquito Springs. But the worst stretch lay between Tule Well and Tinajas Altas—almost twenty waterless miles. Mexican banditos, Anglo desperados, and roaming Hia Ced O'odham preyed on the endless stream of travelers. Hundreds died of thirst. Within the last mile of the life-giving pools at Tinajas Altas, dozens of graves lay marked with crude wooden crosses or heaps of stones.

The first European explorer to pass through this region was Melchior Díaz, a captain in Francisco Vásquez de Coronado's army. Coronado, like other Spanish explorers, was driven by the medieval romance of finding gold-lined streets in the legendary Seven Cities of Cíbola. In 1540, he sent Díaz from Caborca, Mexico, to the Baja coast to meet with the party's supply ships. Accompanied by more than a dozen conquistadors and several Indian guides, Díaz reached the lower Colorado River only to learn that the ships had already departed. On the way back, he was accidentally impaled by his own lance and died somewhere along the trail.

More than 150 years later, the Jesuit priest and explorer Eusebio Francisco Kino arrived on a horse in his long black robes. The padre, whose goal was to expand the so-called rim of Christendom, rounded up the free-roaming indigenes and made them settle in villages. They labored, often against their will, in the hot desert sun, building extravagant missions where they learned to pray to a very different God. In only three years, Kino traveled the entire length of El Camino del Diablo four times. In 1698 and later in 1706, Kino ascended a high volcanic peak in the Pinacate area, looked out beyond the shimmering sand dunes, and was able to see that Baja California was not an island as he had thought, but a peninsula.

Not long after the Gadsden Purchase in 1854, when the land south of the Gila River became part of the United States, miners began straggling into the region. These rugged opportunists staked their claims in mineral outcroppings throughout the monument, dubbing them with lofty names such as Red Warrior, Copper Lion, and Great Bear. There was the Milton Mine in the Puerto Blanco Mountains, named after the colorful lawman that discovered it—Jeff Davis Milton—a former Texas Ranger and the man known as "the first U.S. Border Patrolman." There was also the Lost Cabin Mine in the Sonoyta Mountains, named for a nearby stone house. And, finally, there were the "lady luck" mines, named for wives, friends, and sweethearts such as Maggie, Lilley, Ezra, and Victoria.

Drawn to the area for its silver, gold, copper, and lead, these early prospectors created trails where none had existed before. By night they slept under the stars. By day they drove their picks deep into the earth in search of treasures, abandoning the camps only when the mines failed to yield a profit. Mining continued in the Organ Pipe area until the monument was established in 1937, but it resumed again in 1941 as part of the war effort during World War II. In the 1950s and 1960s, bulldozers replaced the miners' picks, leaving huge scars throughout the desert.

Today, all that remains from "glory holes" such as those at Dripping Springs, as I found on a morning hike, are deep pits surrounded by the weathered beams of wooden shafts. Old litter covers the ground: decomposing cans, broken bottles, and rusted bedsprings where desert pack rats have taken up residence since 1978, when Organ Pipe was declared a wilderness area and mining was finally banned in the monument.

Among the hundreds of claims filed throughout the Organ Pipe area, the Victoria was queen of them all. Located on the eastern lip of the Sonoyta Mountains, the mine once yielded silver, gold, copper, and lead. As one story goes, a California miner and his Cahuilla Indian wife discovered a rich silver vein at the site in about 1880. The two are said to have sold the mine in 1890 to a Mexican bandit-turned-entrepreneur named Cipriano Ortega.

Ortega named the mine La Americana. He claimed to have invested less than $100 in the venture, extracting $14,000 worth of ore, which he crushed with a burro-driven *arrastra*, or grinding mill, at his ranch south of the border. Ortega abandoned the site in the late 1890s, removing the heavy support beams from the mineshaft. In 1899, he sold the dilapidated structure to Mikul G. Levy, a miner and merchant who lived in the area. Levy renamed the mine Victoria after Victoria Leon, the wife of Levy's shopkeeper at Quitobaquito.

In the decades to follow, the Victoria changed hands many times, producing about $30,000 for Levy and only $10,000 for all the miners who followed. Today, the Cipriano Hills, south of the Bates Mountains, honor Cipriano Ortega, who died in 1904 just before a new breed of entrepreneur descended on the Organ Pipe area—the Old West cattle rancher.

In 1919, a Texan named Robert Louis Gray loaded his belongings into a horse-drawn wagon and headed west from Benson, Arizona, to the Mexican town of Sonoyta. As one story goes, Gray's wife, Sara, drove the clumsy carriage across the desert; his sons herded the family's cattle; and Gray himself rode in style in a shiny Model T Ford. The move was inspired when a "For Sale" sign caught Gray's eye in a Tucson bank. The advertisement offered a ranch house, corrals, a windmill, water rights, and three hundred head of cattle along the southern edge of the monument for $5,000. Gray purchased the property from a rancher named Lonald Blankenship, who had scraped out a living on the bleak bajadas of the border country since 1915, the same year that followers of Pancho Villa sought refuge in Bull Pasture during the Mexican Revolution. Known for the six-gun on his hip and his ability to use it, Blankenship had called his homestead Rattlesnake Ranch. Gray preferred a different name.

He called it Dos Lomitas for the two small hills northwest of the ranch. The original ranch house still stands. Its outdoor ramada, whose roof is made of saguaro ribs, faces south toward Mexico a few hundred yards away.

"Cowpunching" had already become established in the area, with ranchers settled at Wall's Well and Dripping Springs. During Prohibition in the early 1930s, some local cowboys and miners bought liquor across the border or became bootleggers, running stills at Diablo and Wildhorse tanks in the Diablo Mountains, at Dripping Springs in the Puerto Blanco Mountains, and at Tinaja Estufa near Kino Peak. They later peddled the moonshine in the nearby town of Ajo. But the largest and most controversial operation in the area was that of Robert Gray and his sons. In the 1920s, Gray's cattle ranged all over the area, grazing on the scanty desert vegetation, exceeding their permit, and leaving the ground barren. Henry Gray, the eldest son, moved from the Dos Lomitas ranch into a small house in Alamo Canyon in 1930, later settling at Bates Well. Jack Gray took over the Alamo Canyon ranch, and his brother Bobby settled at Dowling Well in the Sonoyta hills. At Bonita Well near the Cipriano Hills, the ever-resourceful Grays rigged a corral gate with a large rubber strip from an inner tube. This elastic "trap gate" allowed cattle into the corral, snapping shut behind them and eliminating the need for timely roundups.

The Gray Ranch—present-day Organ Pipe Cactus National Monument—continued to grow in the 1930s. But by the end of the decade the family found itself, much to its dismay, at the center of a long and controversial range war with the federal government. The Taylor Grazing Act of 1934 didn't help; it limited the number of cattle that could graze on public lands. For more than a decade, the Grays' holdings had belonged in a kind of free-for-all public domain. But on April 13, 1937, President Franklin Delano Roosevelt, recognizing the unique desert ecology of the region, declared the area a national monument. In his presidential proclamation, Roosevelt wrote: "Warning is hereby expressly given to all unauthorized persons not to appropriate, injure, destroy, or remove any feature of this monument and not to locate or settle upon any of the lands thereof."

Settlers who had already lived in the area for decades were outraged. In 1943, a homesteader named Birdie Del Miller wrote a letter to Arizona senator Carl Hayden, complaining that "the cactus ranger here is trying to take the place away from me." Later, Henry Gray, who was still living at Bates Well in the northern part of the park, wrote a letter to Senator Barry Goldwater asking permission to retain his water rights. Besides, wrote Gray, "There is not an organ pipe cactus to be seen for as far as the eye can see—with a pair of binoculars—even from the top of a windmill."

The Gray family wielded considerable political clout, and Senator Hayden arranged an initial grazing permit in 1939. The same year, an acting director of the National Park Service denied the Grays a lifetime permit but continued to issue annual permits. In the decades to follow, the Park Service found grazing damage in the area to be extensive. The pressure mounted, and the cowboys soon found themselves at odds with the federal government. By the 1960s, the family was warned that its grazing permit would no longer be renewed, and in the 1970s the Grays were threatened with lawsuits. Finally, Bobby—the last of the Gray brothers—died, marking the end of the conflict and nearly six decades of ranching in the park.

But the damage from grazing had already been done. Roads had been cut and wells drilled throughout the monument. Cattle had trampled and overgrazed the vegetation, causing erosion and upsetting the area's delicate ecology. Finally in 1978, most of the lands that make up Organ Pipe were declared a wilderness area. No longer would ranching or mining be allowed anywhere in the monument. Instead, the fragile desert would begin the task of healing itself.

Morning rings with the song of a white-winged dove. The sky is the color of the sea. Thin white clouds roll above me like low-tide waves. I make a breakfast of granola, pineapple juice, and coffee beneath the saguaros. Then I head back to Quitobaquito to look for yellow warblers, vermilion flycatchers, and, if I'm lucky, a lazuli bunting.

No one is sure exactly what the word *quitobaquito* means. One suggestion is that the term comes from the O'odham language, meaning "a place by the lake where the crowfoot gramma grass grows." Lumholtz believed that quitobaquito came from a Spanish corruption of the O'odham word *alivaipia,* meaning "small springs." Another suggestion is that the name is related to the nearby town of Quitovac about thirty miles south, a place that historian Wilton E. Hoy once described as "a few ruined adobes . . . scattered about the Laguna de Quitobac, a large Quitobaquito-type pond used for irrigation and watering stock." The word *bac* means "watering place" in the O'odham language, and *ito* is the Spanish diminutive for something "small." The site has been occupied for thousands of years, perhaps since the end of the last Ice Age. The Amargosa culture settled in this area five thousand years ago, and for several centuries, the springs were visited by Hohokam shell gatherers and small bands of Tohono and Hia Ced O'odham.

The first written record of the springs comes from Father Kino, who visited the springs in 1698. Kino found a small Indian settlement at Quitobaquito Springs and called the spot San Serguio. Kino, who did not travel lightly, brought with him about 150 head of cattle. Not realizing the damage they might wreak from grazing on the sparse desert grasses, Kino left them at the springs for about a week while he traveled south into the Sierra Pinacate to determine whether Baja was an island or a peninsula. Kino visited Quitobaquito eight times between 1698 and 1706. Other Jesuits, Franciscans, and Spanish soldiers followed. In the 1850s, a small group of Hia Ced O'odham settled at the springs, and Mexican generals, U.S. surveyors, scientists, and prospectors all passed through the area.

In the 1860s, the first American settled at Quitobaquito. Andrew Dorsey, capitalizing on the rare desert springs, dug a pond, built a dam, planted exotic fig and pomegranate trees, and channeled the water though irrigation ditches to water his fields. Dorsey ran a trading post at Quitobaquito, packing in supplies

Gravesite of José Lorenzo Sestier, Quitobaquito cemetery.

by wagon and prospecting for gold in the surrounding hills. It's believed that ore from several nearby mines was milled at Quitobaquito in the 1870s with a burro-driven arrastra.

In 1900, the anthropologist W. J. McGee led an expedition along the Camino del Diablo, stopping briefly at the springs. There he found a few Hia Ced O'odham and the merchant, Levy, who owned the Victoria mine. It's likely that McGee climbed the low hill just north of the pond and visited the grave of a Frenchman named José Lorenzo Sestier, whose tombstone still stands in the Quitobaquito cemetery.

In 1923, President Calvin Coolidge withdrew forty acres around Quitobaquito Springs from the public domain, setting them aside as a Public Water Reserve. In 1957, the National Park Service issued a condemnation agreement with Quitobaquito's last Hia Ced O'odham resident, Jim Orozco. The Service bought his grazing, farming, and squatter's rights for $13,000, but it was already too late. The early settlers at Quitobaquito had severely altered the land and its vegetation. They had dug a pond, built a dam, and planted crops. They had cut wood for fire and shelter in a land of few trees.

Ironically, some of the human disturbances actually helped the wildlife. The shallow, open shore around the pond attracted a number of migrant birds. The cultivated fields drew insects and the birds that fed on them. But cattle grazing had disturbed the native grasses and other plants. The livestock had also trampled the springs themselves and the vegetation associated with them: saltbush, seepweed, yerba mansa, cattail, salt grass, bulrush, and many other plants on which the wildlife depended.

Today, Quitobaquito is slowly beginning to heal. Not long after the cattle were removed in the late 1970s, plants that had been browsed or trampled began to flourish, providing food for pocket mice, kangaroo rats, and ants. The pond and surrounding mesquite thickets now support a large population of breeding birds, including cardinals, orioles, and red-tailed hawks. The pond is also home to rare Sonoyta mud turtles and a number of amphibians. Occasionally, a rattlesnake slithers into one of the shallow ditches leading to the pond, and at times, the tracks of coyotes and kit foxes can be seen in the sand.

One of the most unusual creatures that lives in the pond and springs is the Quitobaquito pupfish, which is thought to be a subspecies of the endangered desert pupfish. Some biologists believe that the desert pupfish has lived in the Southwest for 1.6 million years in a range that included the San Pedro, Santa Cruz, Gila, Salt, and Colorado Rivers and their tributaries in Arizona and California. As the climate warmed, the pupfish became stranded in shallow pools, where it learned to adapt to water hotter than a hundred degrees and three times saltier than the ocean. The pupfish, which measures about two inches in length, feeds on plants, insect larvae, water mites, and even its own eggs. I've watched the species during mating season, when in summer the males turn indigo with bright yellow fins like tropical fish.

Agricultural development in the Sonoyta Valley of Sonora could in time threaten this vulnerable species and the rest of Quitobaquito's ecology. Large-scale irrigation at Mexican *ejidos,* or cooperative farms, could lower the water table at the pond. Pesticides often drift across the border. There are other problems as well. The National Park Service was forced to drain the pond after discovering that golden shiners—a nonnative species that preys on the pupfish—had been released into its waters.

rain

August. I return to Organ Pipe to watch the desert monsoons blow in. The sky is heavy and brooding, the air musty with creosote. Slate-gray clouds advance from the east and cling to the Ajos like cobwebs. Except for the humming of crickets, the desert is so quiet I can hear the blood pounding in my head. Suddenly, a clap of thunder shatters the silence and rumbles westward like the belly of a beast. Rain descends in silver sheets. In minutes the temperature plummets more than thirty degrees, and normally dry arroyos surge with runoff from the mountains.

I stand on the roadside and watch in awe as Kuakatch Wash

cuts a swath fifty feet wide. The rust-colored water moves swiftly and violently, flooding animal burrows and carrying with it tons of debris: sand, silt, rocks, mesquite branches, the nest of a cactus wren, and part of a saguaro. The sky becomes a whiteout. In the diffused light, the spines of a barrel cactus turn scarlet. The pale green bark of a palo verde resembles velvet. Beads of water hang from its branches, reflecting the world upside-down. At sunset, salmon clouds form to the west, turning crimson then violet. To the south in Mexico, twin rainbows rise from the earth, and somewhere beyond, a tiny patch of blue breaks through the clouds and is quickly swallowed.

The desert becomes a living carpet as thousands of small black worms crawl along the ground and up into bushes. They're desert millipedes, also known as "rain worms." The millipede is not an insect, but is more closely related to lobsters, crayfish, and shrimp. This two-inch-long creature lives most of the year below ground, often in the burrows or nests of other desert dwellers. It comes out when it rains to gorge on dead leaves, cactus, and the bark of shrubs. I try not to step on them.

The giant desert centipede also emerges from its home under rocks and prowls the desert floor for insects. Near the Visitor's Center, I find one that has drowned in a rain puddle, and I squat down to examine it. Its orange and black body is about eight inches long. It has bright yellow legs and long yellow antennae. Despite its name, it has only forty-two legs. The front of its body bears a pair of poison fangs, which are used to strike prey such as insects and spiders. Contrary to some stories, its legs aren't venomous, but its bite can be painful to humans.

Everything here depends on rain. Between November and April, gentle winter rains carried in low-pressure systems arrive from the Pacific Ocean, seeping into the soil and helping seeds germinate. Spectacular displays of spring wildflowers occur only during "wet" years, about once or twice in a decade, drawing up to 400,000 visitors to the park. For this to happen, a special sequence of events must take place in winter: generous rains that soften seed coats; followed by mild weather, which promotes germination; and finally, a good rain or two in February or March. If these conditions are present, the results can be astonishing, as I would see one spring: tapestries of Mexican gold poppies, purple owl's clover, and white desert dandelions.

One of the most stunning spring wildflowers here is the Ajo lily, which grows in the sand and resembles the Easter lilies I grow in my garden. The Tohono O'odham once harvested its bulbs as an important food source. It's believed that the early Spanish explorers called the bulbs *ajo,* the word for garlic, because of their taste. (Garlic is a member of the lily family.)

Hedgehog, cholla, and prickly pear cactus also bloom in spring, as do the large columnar cacti: organ pipe, saguaro, and senita. Then in summer, between July and September, thunderstorms arrive on tongues of moist air from the Gulf of Mexico. In only a few short weeks, these storms drop about half the annual rainfall on the monument. Most of the runoff flows north, or becomes groundwater. Here in the Sonoran Desert, most arroyos flow only a few times a year. Yet in those fleeting hours, an entire cycle of life is set into motion. The dormant ocotillo sprouts dark green leaves, and the creosote bush blooms once again. Small patches of summer annuals appear: yellow chinchweed, golden poppies, and scarlet spiderlings. In only a few short weeks these delicate flowers will die, but their tiny seeds, so vibrant in their will to survive, will lie dormant in the soil awaiting moisture.

This is exactly how the spadefoot toad adapts to drought. The toad burrows underground and remains there for nine or ten months in a torpid state. When thunder rumbles over the mountains, the spadefoot responds by emerging from its burrow to mate. I once watched one by lantern light after a heavy rain. It was sitting on a rock, rolling its tongue out like a yo-yo and catching more moths than I could count. The ultimate challenge for the toad is to reproduce quickly in shallow pools after the summer rains. To meet this challenge, the spadefoot develops very quickly. Its eggs hatch in only a few days, and the tadpoles mature in only a couple weeks. Once the puddles have dried up, the toad will be ready to burrow into the earth by using the hardened spades on its hind feet and will stay there to await the summer rains.

The scorpion also loves moisture and can easily be found during the summer monsoons. This arthropod is the descendant of a long lineage that dates back 400 million years and lives mostly in small burrows beneath rocks and soil debris. Some hide under the bark of trees—or the ground cloths of unsuspecting campers. When stinging its prey, the scorpion flashes its venomous tail forward over its eight-legged body and strikes with a hypodermic-like stinger. The unlucky insect, spider, or other scorpion is then eaten—head first. Adult scorpions are loners, except while mating. The young are born alive in thin sacs. Once they break through these sacs, they climb onto their mother's back and ride around—high and dry—until strong enough to make it on their own. Scorpions are fluorescent: you can watch them in darkness with a black light.

Early one morning I observe one of the oddest spectacles in the desert. A big hairy tarantula that has begun to molt emerges from its burrow near a fallen saguaro. Seeing this, a red and black wasp alights on the spider and stings it, sending it into spasms. The wasp, known as a tarantula hawk, then drags its victim by the leg into a shallow burrow, where it lays a single egg upon its body and covers the spider with dirt. In the weeks to come, the larva will feast on the still-living tarantula, until it pupates and hatches into a single adult wasp.

Desert tarantulas also love moisture and come out to mate. I've seen them by the hundreds during the summer rains, crawling across the desert in search of mates—or flattened by passing cars on Arizona Highway 85, which runs north and south through the monument. The tarantula is the largest spider of the desert with a leg span of up to four inches. When it finds prey, the tarantula jumps on it and strikes with venomous fangs. It grinds the victim into a ball, secretes digestive enzymes on it through its fangs to liquefy it, then sucks it up. The tarantula lives in burrows lined with silk produced by spinnerets. It does not weave a web to capture prey, but pursues it by foot in the darkness of night. Female tarantulas can live up to twenty-five years. Despite a number of myths, no tarantula in the United States has a bite that is deadly to humans. If provoked, the spider can leave a bite similar to that of a wasp sting (which might spur an allergic reaction). In fact, the gentle tarantula is reluctant to attack people at all; it will crawl across a hand or an arm without biting, as schoolchildren discover, to the delight of all but the most squeamish, at demonstrations at the Arizona-Sonora Desert Museum in Tucson. The tarantula is so fragile that if dropped, it can shatter. When startled by a predator, the tarantula might show its fangs, or rub its sides with its hind legs, releasing a spray of fine hairs, which are irritating to the eyes or mucous membranes of small creatures. The tarantula feeds on insects, lizards, and other spiders. In turn, it is eaten by rodents, birds, lizards, and some kinds of snakes.

By October, the desert once again enters a dry spell. Arroyos that once surged with runoff become ribbons of sand. With the rainy season now over, the tarantula returns to its burrow, the millipede crawls back into the softened earth, and the spadefoot toad—the true symbol of desert rain—remains underground in an altered state until thunder rolls over the land and the rain begins again.

cactus country

A bright honey moon rises in the east over the mountains. The light illuminates the desert below, turning my skin an iridescent blue. I examine my hands, wondering how other creatures perceive me in the dark. They must hear me. Surely, they can see me. The desert itself is eerily quiet; the only sound is the wind whistling through the spines of the saguaros. I lie on my sleeping bag in Seven Saguaro Camp observing their tall silhouettes long into the night. Sometimes they resemble totem poles reaching into the sky. Other times they look like people with outstretched arms, waving to one another across the Valley of the Ajo. The Tohono O'odham call the cactus *ha:sañ,* and consider it a sacred relative. According to O'odham legend, the first saguaro was created when a young maiden sank into the earth and arose as a giant cactus with arms raised up to the heavens.

The saguaro is the largest cactus in the United States and can live to be one of the oldest: about 200 years. Surprisingly, of the 40 million seeds the cactus produces in its lifetime, only one or two survive the seedling state to reach maturity. Against those odds, it's a wonder this giant desert matriarch survives at all. But the saguaro is a nucleus of life in the complex web of desert ecology. Its graceful arms bear ivory blossoms that attract bees, insects, doves, and bats—especially the lesser long-nosed bat, an endangered species and the primary nighttime pollinator of the cactus. Once the flowers have shriveled and died in the hot desert sun, green egg-shaped fruits appear, ripening and turning red. Only a few hours after the fruits have fallen to the ground and split open, harvester ants carry away the seeds and store them underground. Kangaroo rats, pocket mice, ground squirrels, javelinas, and coyotes scavenge the fruits. White-winged doves gorge on the fruit and excrete the seeds throughout the desert. The seeds germinate during the rainy season in July and August.

The Tohono and Hia Ced O'odham maintain cultural ties with the monument and sometimes go there to gather organ pipe and saguaro fruit. In parts of the Sonoran Desert during Hasan Bakmasad in June (saguaro moon), the O'odham nudge fruit down from the saguaro with thirty-foot-long poles made of dry saguaro ribs. The fruit is then placed in large earthenware ollas and boiled down. As the liquid ferments into wine, the O'odham dance around the jars as they have for centuries.

Come and sing!
Come and sing!
Sing for the evening!
The sun stands there.
Sing for it!
For the liquor, delightfully sing
delightfully sing!

The liquor is made.
The liquor is made.
It is set.
Come to sing!
Now shortly it will foam.

This is the Tohono O'odham New Year's celebration, when the people conduct a sacred wine ceremony passed down by I'itoi, "Elder Brother." For days, they dance, sing rain songs, recite cloud poems, drink large quantities of the wine, and regurgitate the liquor in a ritual known as "throwing up the clouds."

The O'odham believe that the more beautiful their songs, the more the rain will come.

Above emerged a huge white cloud.
With its head against the sky it stood;
Then it began to move.

Although the earth seemed very wide,
Clear to the edge of it it went.

From within the great rainy mountains
Rushed out a huge black cloud
And joined with it.
Pulling out their white breast feathers they went;
Spreading their white breast feathers far and
Wide they went;
Then they stood still and saw

They saw the earth lie beautifully moist and
   Finished
Upon it came forth seed,
And a thick root came forth;
And well they ripened.
There were delightful evenings,
Delightful the dawns.

Not long after the cloud-calling ceremony ends, the rain begins, setting the life cycle of the saguaro—and everything else—into motion once again.

After about one year, the tiny saguaro seedling is about the size of a pea and can easily be trampled by a careless hiking boot. At fifteen years, it is about two inches high. At fifty, the saguaro reaches about three feet and begins producing its first blossoms. At seventy-five it soars to about eight feet, and arms begin to sprout from its trunk. In its first few years, the saguaro faces a number of obstacles: heat, frost, floods, droughts, and rodents, some of which can chew off the spines of the cactus and gnaw into its tender flesh. Often a seedling will thrive beneath the shelter of a "nurse tree," which provides a barrier to animals and protection from the heat. Nurse plants include small shrubs and desert trees such as mesquite, ironwood, and palo verde. In a sense, the nurse plant gives up its life for the cactus: the remains of these trees can often be found beneath a saguaro like a heap of sun-bleached bones.

The mature saguaro usually lives in a dense saguaro "forest." It can grow to a height of sixty feet, weigh nine tons, and support up to fifty arms. The saguaro provides shelter for a number of bird species. Gila woodpeckers and gilded flickers peck holes into the saguaro's trunk or arms to build nests, turning it into a gigantic birdhouse. Once the excavators move out, other birds, such as elf and screech owls, move in. The astute desert wanderer will sometimes notice high up in the arms of a saguaro the scraggly nest of a red-tailed hawk. These nests are happily claimed later by ravens, great horned owls, and Cooper's hawks.

Saguaros breathe. Listen.

First light. A soft breeze tumbles down from the mountains, dissipating in the valley below. My destination this morning is the broad bajadas in the Ajo Mountains, where the organ pipe thrives on the sunniest slopes. The cactus is in bloom now, and I drive east into the foothills, stopping at a turnout to investigate a twenty-foot-high specimen. Delicate white flowers, tinged with pink, have sprouted from its dark green arms. A fuzzy

Gila woodpecker and organ pipe cactus blossom.

bumblebee pokes its head into a newly opened blossom, and a small red spider floats down on an invisible strand of silk.

Next to the saguaro, the organ pipe is the second-largest columnar cactus in the United States. It has been prized by Sonoran Desert cultures since it first arrived here four thousand years ago. Its ribs have been used to make torches, cooking utensils, and shelters such as brush houses and open-air ramadas. The fruit can be eaten as is, or made into jam, or fermented into wine. The Seri Indians mixed its rind and spongy pith with animal fat to make a caulking material for boats. In Mexico, the plant is called *pitahaya dulce,* "sweet cactus," because of its succulent fruit.

Yet, as generous as the cactus is, it's also vulnerable. Frost that settles on the desert floor can damage its tips and stunt its growth. One key to the plant's survival in the monument lies in its stems. To adjust to the cooler climate here, the cactus has developed thicker stems than those of its sisters in Mexico, keeping it warmer.

The chief pollinator of the cactus is the lesser long-nosed bat—the only nectar-feeding bat in the monument. This tiny mammal roosts in rock crevices and decrepit mine shafts. It comes out at night to feed on organ pipe and saguaro blossoms. Organ pipe flowers open after the sun goes down and close the next morning. Yet in this very short time, something magical takes place. In the darkness of night, the bat flits from flower to flower, taking in nectar, pollinating the male and female parts of the cactus, and assuring its survival.

Frost-damaged organ pipe cactus, La Abra Plain.

On a bright day in May, I head out for Aguajita Wash, on the western side of the monument, in search of smoke trees and other unfamiliar plants. Each species here has its own special ecology, and I soon realize that the more I learn, the less I know. Why is a smoke tree called a smoke tree? For its plumelike growth, which gives the tree the appearance of smoke—until bright purple blossoms sprout from its branches. When I find the trees, they're not yet flowering, so I drive east along the dirt road that parallels the international border fence. Soon I turn north into Senita Basin, one of the most vibrant pockets of the monument and home to a very rare cactus: the senita. I find it where the dirt road ends. Thin gray whiskers, some nearly two inches long, sprout from the tips of its stems. These "whiskers" are actually spines, and nothing looks as peculiar as the fragile pink flowers that bloom on this shaggy cactus in May. Most senitas in the basin are small compared to those in Mexico. Here at the northern limit of their range, they are in fact struggling to survive in the cooler climate. The entire U.S. population of senitas is found only in a few isolated pockets in the monument.

I spend the rest of the day hiking down abandoned mining roads and looking at elephant trees, so named because the base of their scaly gray trunk resembles an elephant's foot. Near an old mesquite tree, I come upon a herd of javelinas grazing on prickly pear cactus—spines and all—softly snorting as they eat. They're bristly gray with elongated snouts. Startled by my sudden appearance, they bark and cough before scattering into the brush.

In the afternoon I watch dozens of black vultures stream in from the east and roost in a cluster of saguaros as they do every day. The vultures have been away hunting for carrion. They look awkward with their puny heads and beady eyes, yet there's a gracefulness to their movements—the way they circle the desert without ever seeming to flap their wings.

It's getting hotter as the sun arcs south, and my shirt is soaked with sweat. I pour water on my bandana and tie it around my head to stay cool. The water in my plastic bottle is so hot that if I dropped a tea bag in I would have sun tea. Perhaps if I paid closer attention to how other creatures adapt here in the heat, I might find it easier to get by. As a human being, though, I nurse thoughts of air-conditioning and an ice-cold margarita. But still I persist—which is all that this place asks of me.

adaptation

S mells are good at releasing memories, and just as sweet clover and dandelion unleash my childhood days in rural northern Japan, the musty odor of creosote takes me back to the desert's soul. This dark green shrub with bright yellow flowers is the most common plant in the park and one of the most drought-resistant perennials in the Sonoran Desert. It is also quite possibly one of the oldest living things on earth. Based on radio-carbon dating of a plant in the Mojave Desert, it is believed that the oldest living creosote is nearly 12,000 years old, making it one of the first life forms to colonize the Mojave.

I've seen creosote bush in three of the major North American deserts, all except the Great Basin—that vast sea of sagebrush and rattlesnake weed. Perhaps the wind carried creosote seeds to the Sonoran Desert, or perhaps migrating birds brought them north from South America where the plant originated. The shrub adapts well to stress, using elaborate defenses and surviving at times without rain for years at a time. Its waxy leaves reduce evaporation. During severe drought, the plant turns brown, dropping most of its foliage and replacing it with tougher leaves. A more curious survival tactic is the poison creosote bush creates and circulates into the soil through its roots. This discourages competitive plants from taking root nearby. Some chemicals in creosote's resin taste so terrible they repel would-be grazers. Many of the plant's compounds are simply indigestible.

Yet the creosote is said to hold great promise today as a pharmaceutical drug, and its medicinal properties did not go unnoticed centuries ago by native peoples. In Tohono O'odham cosmology, Earth Maker tossed soil from his breast, and creosote was the first thing to sprout. The Tohono O'odham call the shrub *cikoi*. Traditionally, they used the plant for everything from coughs and bruises, to bladder stones, menstrual cramps, rheumatism, snakebites, and stinky feet. Today, chemists are studying the curative powers of creosote bush. An extract from the shrub has been found to kill human cancer cells in laboratory test tubes.

Here in the Sonoran Desert, the strategies for survival are as varied as there are species of plants. One of the most successful trees is the mesquite, a member of the pea family whose name comes from the Aztec Nahuatl word *mizquitl*. The tree normally grows along arroyos and avoids drought by sending out a long taproot, sometimes fifty feet deep when groundwater is present. Its seeds germinate only after heavy summer rains, and its tender roots must race down to permanent groundwater before the summer heat sets in. Like creosote, the mesquite is a traditional desert pharmacy. Its bark has been used to fight bladder infections, measles, and fevers; its branches and stems are used as a purgative. Its pods can be used to make eyewash and as a poultice for sore throat; its gum for infections, lice and hemorrhoids; its leaves for headaches, diarrhea, and red ant stings. Native Americans eat the pods and make candy, dye, and glue out of the sap. Some properties of the plant are even used to treat type 2 diabetes because they stabilize blood sugar.

In Spanish, *palo verde* means "green stick," a name given to this desert tree for its smooth green bark. Also a member of the pea family, the palo verde puts out tiny green leaves in spring. Most of the photosynthesis, though, occurs in the bark to conserve moisture. Two species grow in the park: the blue palo verde and the foothills palo verde, and in spring, their blossoms burnish the desert with gold.

The ocotillo has a different strategy for getting by. In the spring, after the winter rains have passed, waxy green leaves and tubular red flowers sprout along its spiny arms. As the days get hotter, the ocotillo drops its leaves to conserve water, standing there like a clump of lifeless sticks. But about thirty-six hours after a rain, small green leaves magically appear on its whiplike branches. In the Sonoran Desert, indigenous cultures and Mexican campesinos often plant ocotillo stems around their homes and corrals. The thorny stems become living fences as green leaves emerge after the rains. The ocotillo can support up to one hundred branches. It can grow thirty feet tall and live for more than sixty years. Often mistaken for a cactus, the ocotillo is actually an ancient relative of the boojum tree—a bizarre-looking plant that resembles an upside-down carrot.

By far, the most adaptable desert plants are the cacti. Succulents such as the organ pipe, saguaro, and senita avoid drought by absorbing water rapidly through shallow root systems. They store this moisture in tissue in their stems, using it sparingly during droughts. At night, the plants open their stomata to take up carbon dioxide. At dawn, they close these pores for the rest of the day to conserve moisture.

Desert wildlife has its own way of adapting to the heat, and if evolution is the key to survival, the kangaroo rat is the epitome of the desert-adapted mammal. Known as "the rodent that never drinks water," this tiny creature has no sweat glands; it cools off by breathing. Its urine is five times more concentrated than that of humans, its kidneys so highly advanced that it seldom urinates. The rodent, which resembles a gerbil, lives in sandy soils throughout the park. It feeds mostly on dry seeds, converting them into water. As its name implies, the kangaroo rat can perform impressive pirouettes, leaping almost two feet in any direction, including straight up. Its ears are so sensitive that it can even hear the flapping of owl wings or the scraping of snake scales in the sand.

The desert tortoise is the next best water miser. It can live

Entwined saguaro and organ pipe cactus, Grass Canyon.

where ground temperatures exceed 140 degrees by digging a burrow to escape the heat. I've seen it in the park, grazing on cactus pads, and if enough rain has fallen, on wildflowers and grass. The tortoise stores moisture in a bladder inside the upper section of its shell and can survive more than a year without drinking water. Its armored skin and hard carapace guard against predators such as ravens, roadrunners, and coyotes, and prevent precious fluids from evaporating. During dry spells, the tortoise keeps cool by digging a tunnel and remaining in this humid environment for most of the day. It mates in summer, usually after a sparring match in which two males nip, ram, and attempt to flip each other over. The tortoise can grow more than a foot long and live to the venerable age of eighty.

Unlike the plodding tortoise, the antelope jackrabbit can travel at speeds of up to thirty-five miles an hour when pursued by a predator. The jackrabbit has evolved some curious survival strategies: its eight-inch-long ears transfer heat away from its body and radiate it into the air. This cooling system only works if the jackrabbit is facing away from the sun. Conversely, on cold winter days, the rabbit faces the sun to absorb heat through its ears. Even more startling is its ability to change colors with the blink of an eye. Called "flashing," this trick is used to outsmart predators. As it zigzags across the desert, the rabbit uses the sleek muscles in its hindquarters to expose a white underfur, helping it escape by confounding pursuers.

Reptiles have their own ways of adapting as I would often see while hiking up an arroyo. The sidewinder is aptly named for the way it loops its body sideways, leaving a signature of

Common collared lizard, Bull Pasture Trail.

S-shaped patterns in the sand. Called "sandwalking," this tactic is used to avoid contact with hot sand, or to prevent slipping on unstable ground. The sidewinder is also known as the "horned rattlesnake" because of the pointed bumps that protrude over its eyes. It preys on lizards and rodents. In turn, it is preyed upon by raptors or by the whimsical roadrunner—a desert cuckoo that can run at speeds of up to seventeen miles an hour and is one of the few creatures that will actually attack a rattlesnake. It does this by seizing the snake by the tail, snapping it like a whip, and slamming its diamond-shaped head into the ground until it dies.

The chuckwalla and desert iguana are far less hostile. They're herbivores that eat flowers, leaves, and fruit, and laze around in the sun, even when the temperature is more than 100 degrees. The chuckwalla is a relative of the tropical green iguana that evolved after the Baja peninsula split from the Mexican mainland about 4 million years ago. Once I surprised a chuckwalla on the Bull Pasture Trail in the Ajo Mountains. It looked like a tiny gray dinosaur. Assuming I was a predator, it wedged itself between two rocks and inflated its body like a big fat balloon. This is one defense the reptile uses to survive by day. Night creatures have their own ways of adapting.

night moves

Why is it that we often feel a connection while gazing at the stars? Our bodies contain hydrogen, carbon, and oxygen— elements that came from the Big Bang that created the universe between ten and twenty billion years ago. We are, in fact, stardust that sifted down into the ocean, morphed, and eventually crawled out of that churning cauldron. At night from my camp-site in the saguaros, I watch the stars emerge like a million eyes and ponder where we came from. Meteorites sail by to the east over the Ajos, leaving long green tails as they go.

In the heat of the day, all seems infinitely still, but here in darkness, the world suddenly comes alive. Rodents crawl from their burrows to feed. Scorpions and tarantulas go hunting. Bats flit around camp searching for moths. Most likely these bats are western pipistrelles, the common ones I see at twilight, and one of at least a dozen species of bats in the park. They include the big brown bat, which often roosts in rock crevices or in holes in saguaros, and the pallid bat, found in the western part of the monument. Bats aren't blind; they see only in black and white. They're highly evolved flying mammals that locate insects by emitting low-frequency sound waves; in flight, a bat can produce thirty or more ultrasonic cries per second. The sound waves bounce off trees and rocks, traveling back to the bat and alerting it to obstacles in its path—or to tasty night-flying bugs; it can eat half its weight in insects in a single night. Some evenings in camp I worry that a bat will get tangled in my hair while chasing an insect and bite my scalp in a frantic attempt to escape. But I love watching these tiny mammals flit around, topsy-turvy, as though writing calligraphy in the air.

What a bat can hear, an owl can see. The great horned owl has keen night vision, so keen in fact that many cultures believe it has supernatural powers. Its strong wings, sometimes spanning five feet, help it swoop down on an unsuspecting rodent, a rabbit, or even a skunk. It has feathered ear tufts or "horns," which help the owl hear what it might not see. At night, I often listen to one hooting from its perch in a nearby saguaro. It's one of the classic sounds of the desert.

On dark summer nights, rattlesnakes also emerge from their shelters. At least two dozen species of snakes live in the monument; they play a vital role in the ecosystem by controlling rodents.

The western diamondback is the largest and most prevalent snake in the Sonoran Desert and can grow about four or five feet long. The rattlesnake produces venom in specialized glands. Heat-sensing pits on the sides of its head help it locate prey, and its forked tongue picks up odors and transfers them to a special organ in the roof of its mouth. The snake's double-hinged jaw allows it to swallow prey bigger than its own body, including kangaroo rats, birds, and scaly lizards.

Each year, about a thousand people are bitten by rattlesnakes in the United States, most of them after intentionally disturbing the snakes. Yet contrary to undying legend, few bites are fatal. In fact, about 98 percent of people bitten by a rattler live to tell about it. I'm one of them, having startled a rattler once while hiking alone in the Tucson Mountains. It was a "dry bite," though, and I managed to walk out of there and drive myself home.

Among the many species of snakes found at Organ Pipe are the black racer and gopher snake, both of which can crawl up a cholla and rob the nest of a cactus wren; the Mojave rattler, one of the most venomous; the Yuma king snake, which commonly feeds on other snakes; and the Arizona coral snake, a secretive and nonaggressive member of the cobra family with bright rings of yellow, red, and black.

Alamo Canyon. I lie awake in my tent listening to coyotes communicate across the hillsides. Sometimes their yips, yaps, and howls come in erratic spurts, and other times their high-pitched songs echo down the arroyo. This trickster of American Indian folklore is an omnivore: it eats just about anything, including rabbits, rodents, and occasionally a diseased or dying deer. The coyote is also a scavenger, feeding on dead animals, usually roadkills. It eats a variety of plants, including wild or domestic melons, roots, berries, even grass. Males assist the females in raising the young, which are fed regurgitated food. The wily coyote has been observed in some parts of the desert with its nocturnal friend, the badger. In fact, symbols of the two appear together on prehistoric Indian pottery. The coyote is known to share part of its catch with the badger. In exchange, the faithful badger frightens rodents from their burrows for the ready-to-pounce coyote.

Outside my tent now as the coyotes grow silent and the moon rises over Montezuma's Head, something scuttles over the rocks, dislodging a few pebbles as it goes. It clangs through my cooking pot and pokes around at my spoon. I'm afraid to peer out, but when I do, I see that it's only a young ringtail cat. It has short pointed ears, a wet pink nose, and a bushy, black-and-white banded tail. When I shine my flashlight into its foxlike eyes, it is more terrified than I am.

In Latin, the ringtail is called *Bassariscus astutus*, "cunning little fox." But this furry creature is neither a fox nor a cat. It's the most primitive member of the raccoon family: it evolved some 13 million years ago. At night, the ringtail forages on plants, mice, insects, and birds, and sometimes the leftover food of campers. The shy creature lives in brushy arroyos and rock shelters in the park. At times, it claims abandoned line shacks and cabins. Early prospectors in the area once kept it as a "pet" because it was so good at controlling rodents.

Bobcat bones, Ajo Mountains.

Among the true cats in the park are the bobcat and the mountain lion. The bobcat spends its days sheltered in brushy thickets or in rock crevices. If approached by a human, it will usually lie perfectly still to escape detection. If forced to flee, it will bolt erratically to the nearest refuge. In stalking its prey, the bobcat crouches patiently, waiting to capture a rabbit, mouse, bird, or even a young deer. During mating season the male fills the canyons with eerie, deafening howls. He takes no part in providing food for the kittens. In fact, the female boots him out of the den and sends him slouching through the cactus.

life on the edge

On a single summer evening, the large white flowers of the night-blooming cereus open, are pollinated, and die with the rising sun.

This fragile cactus, difficult to detect even for those who are familiar with it, resembles a dead stick poking out of the sand, as I would see one day in the Bates Mountains while searching for petroglyphs. But its large white blossoms, among the most elegant and fragrant of any cactus, have earned it the name "queen of the night." When darkness falls, the flowers are pollinated by bats, birds, and insects, chief among them the night-flying hawk moth. The moth flits from flower to flower, transferring the golden pollen to the stigma of other blossoms. The plants have large, water-storing taproots, which can weigh more than eighty pounds. These edible tubers attracted Native Americans long ago, who located them by following the intoxicating scent of the flowers throughout the desert.

In Arizona, the night-blooming cereus, like many other desert plants, is protected by law. The list includes all cacti, agaves, and yuccas. All wildlife is also protected from disturbance in a national park or monument, and several species here are federally endangered. Among them are the Sonoran pronghorn, the cactus ferruginous pygmy owl, the lesser long-nosed bat, and the Quitobaquito pupfish.

The Sonoran pronghorn was listed as endangered in 1967. Its scientific name is *Antilocapra americana sonoriensis,* "American-Sonoran antelope goat." But the pronghorn is neither antelope nor goat. This rare and skittish creature is a subspecies of pronghorn. Here in the Sonoran Desert, it's smaller and lighter in color—buff with a white belly and black stripes on its face and neck. A lucky visitor at Organ Pipe can sometimes see a pronghorn galloping gracefully at fifty or sixty miles an hour on the western side of the park. Today, only about twenty-one Sonoran pronghorns exist in the United States, a drop from 140 animals in 1998. The population crashed after a prolonged drought at the turn of the millennium when the rain didn't fall for nearly a year. The same die-out occurred across the border in Mexico. Today, only fifteen or twenty pronghorn survive in the sand dunes east of Puerto Peñasco, where winter dew provides more moisture. The entire U.S. population lives in Organ

Pipe, the Cabeza Prieta National Wildlife Refuge west of the park, and the adjacent Barry M. Goldwater Range, where the Department of Defense conducts bombing practice, aerial gunnery, rocketry, ground maneuvers, and electronic warfare. All of these activities can have a dramatic impact on the species. So can hungry coyotes, bobcats, and mountain lions; competition with cattle for grasses; and fragmentation of the pronghorn's range by highways and barbed wire fences. The pronghorn is also threatened by an enormous wave of undocumented immigrants moving north through its habitat, the constant movement of Border Patrol vehicles and helicopters, and sonic booms from the gunnery range. In a last-ditch rescue effort, wildlife biologists are conducting a captive breeding program to save this sensitive species from extinction.

In 1976, the United Nations declared Organ Pipe Cactus National Monument an International Biosphere Reserve. As such, the monument became the world's first representative of the Sonoran Desert under a UNESCO (United Nations Educational, Scientific, and Cultural Organization) program called Man and the Biosphere. The project is designed to study the region's biodiversity and the human impact on the area's ecology, to foster wise use of the resources, and to preserve it for future generations.

The designation was a milestone, yet the very next year, in 1977, another species was added to the endangered list: the cactus ferruginous pygmy owl. The owl is a small, reddish-brown bird with yellow eyes. It nests in cavities in saguaros and organ pipes, or in arroyos where ironwood, palo verde, and mesquite trees grow. Fewer than fifty known adult owls now live in Arizona; only a few pairs now roost in Organ Pipe monument.

In 1986, the Quitobaquito pupfish also made the list. The only healthy populations of desert pupfish in the Sonoran Desert survive in Quitobaquito Springs and the Cienega Santa Clara across the border in Mexico. Today, an estimated four to five thousand pupfish survive in their namesake pond in the monument. Some of the greatest threats to this vulnerable little species are clogging of the stream channel to the pond; pesticides from aerial spraying at ejidos, or Mexican cooperative farms; and trash dumping along Mexican Highway 2, which runs just south of the pond.

In 1988, the lesser long-nosed bat, formerly known as Sanborn's long-nosed bat, joined the others as endangered when it was learned that only a few hundred of the mammals remained in Arizona. The bat is the primary nighttime pollinator of the organ pipe and saguaro. It assures their survival by transferring pollen from flower to flower. The bat also pollinates the agave— the plant that's distilled to make tequila. Agricultural pesticides, livestock grazing, and a huge foreign taste for margaritas have taken their toll on the agave—and therefore the bat.

But much greater threats exist than these, as I would see on my next visit to the park.

under siege

There's always a risk in returning to a place we love, and in the summer of 2003, I come back to Organ Pipe with photographer Michael Hyatt and my friend John Russial to document some of the changes taking place throughout the park. Henry David Thoreau once wrote: "Things do not change, we change." But as I arrive here, I can see that things *have* changed. I remember this desert as though it were yesterday: the fleeting clouds, the emptiness of the land, the great silence that settles over the desert like breath. These qualities are timeless, but I am quite unprepared for what I see now.

At the northern entrance to the park, eighty-foot-high surveillance towers rise above the desert with cameras so powerful they can read a license plate two miles away. Government vehicles, driven by armed agents from the U.S. Border Patrol, the Drug Enforcement Agency (DEA), and the Bureau of Customs and Border Protection, appear everywhere as part of the post–9/11 Department of Homeland Security.

The monument has also become the frontline in a war zone to stop drug smugglers. Drug trafficking has occurred in Organ Pipe for decades, but lately things have gotten much worse. Many smugglers no longer hike up remote canyons with pot-filled backpacks. They cross through the border fence in powerful four-wheel-drive vehicles, carry AK-47s, use night-vision equipment, and wear body armor. They station people on the hilltops as lookouts and use portable solar panels to power their radios. They light the dry stems of chollas on fire to create diversions and sometimes topple saguaros as roadblocks.

Against these well-armed, well-equipped smugglers stand the U.S. Park Service rangers of Organ Pipe, who now dress in full camouflage and carry M16s. They use two-way radios, motion detectors, and infrared scopes, and they carry plastic handcuffs.

On any given night it's estimated that one to two thousand people pass through the park into the United States illegally— more than the number that enter legally. These include drug runners and "coyotes"—people who smuggle migrants across the border for a fee and often abandon them in the blazing sun. Every summer, migrants who come seeking a better life in "El Norte" die by the hundreds from dehydration along the U.S.–

Migrants passing through Puerto Blanco Mountains.

Mexican border. At times, some of these migrants have died within the park's boundaries.

The constant foot traffic has carved more than a hundred miles of illegal trails throughout the park. Cars, trucks, bicycles, handcarts, and sport-utility vehicles (SUVs) have left tracks in what was once a quiet wilderness. The constant passage of people and vehicles has affected endangered species such as the pygmy owl, which abandons its nest if disturbed by humans. Names of travelers and towns have been carved into 150-year-old saguaros or spray-painted on rock walls. Contemporary sleeping circles have been built near ancient ones, and new rock cairns on ancient trails confuse hikers. Mesquite trees have been cut with machetes for firewood. Campfires have been lit and abandoned. Rare plants such as the night-blooming cereus have been dug up and stolen for their medicinal properties. Clothing has been shed and discarded beneath the meager shade of palo verde trees. Mexican comic books and baby diapers cling to the spines of prickly pear cactus. Bibles, rattlesnake antivenin bottles, plastic water jugs, and food cans litter the ground by the ton along with human feces. The only way to remove the trash is by hand.

Lately, those passing through have become more difficult to track. The smarter ones brush away their footprints with creosote branches. In effect, Organ Pipe's rangers have been forced to become de facto agents for the Border Patrol, Customs, and the DEA. The paradox is that by increasing law enforcement in the park, there is less protection for the natural and cultural resources, which is why this national monument was created in the first place.

On a bright August morning in 2002, Organ Pipe ranger Kris Eggle rose early as usual. He jogged down a desert trail as he did every single morning, past the ocotillos and saguaros. When he got home, he showered, then put on a Kevlar vest and a camouflage uniform. It was going to be hot today, 110 degrees at least. The vest made it worse. Eggle would be doing what he did any other day in the monument—inspecting the border fence, checking up on the resources, and keeping an eye out for people traveling through the park illegally. For the twenty-eight-year-old high school valedictorian and cross-country runner, it was just another day.

That afternoon, Eggle and a U.S. Border Patrol agent heard a radio report that Mexican authorities had pursued two drug runners wanted for murder in Mexico. The fugitives had stolen an SUV and sped through a fifteen-foot hole in the border fence into the park. The SUV had gotten stuck in a sandy arroyo. Eggle and the agent drove to the scene, pulled over, and ran toward the vehicle. When three other Border Patrol agents arrived to help, one of the fugitives threw down his gun and was captured. The other man fled into the brush. Eggle pursued him. Three shots rang out from an AK-47. One round hit Eggle's radio, ricocheted up under his Kevlar vest, and sliced through his femoral artery. The shooter ran southeast toward the border, where dozens of Mexican police waited on the other side. In a scene that could have come from *Butch Cassidy and the Sundance Kid,* a fusillade of more than two hundred bullets cut the fugitive down.

Humane Borders volunteer Monica Zavala-Durazo, Valley of the Ajo.

Park ranger Kris Eggle died before an ambulance could get him to a hospital.

The incident has renewed a long debate on how to better protect the U.S. border. On one hand, armed military guards, lookout towers, and searchlights might protect the resources and those who guard them. On the other, such drastic measures might diminish the wilderness experience for visitors who do not want their national parks turned into battlefields.

A new border fence made of railroad steel might hinder vehicles trying to enter the park illegally, but not the great majority of people who enter by foot, hoping to find work in the fields and orchards of the American West. Often they come without enough water to make it across the desert. Volunteers now run water stations in and around the park where parched migrants can fill their jugs. Dozens of beacons have also been erected throughout the park, where those in trouble can push a help button to summon a search and rescue team.

All of this activity has taken its toll. Threats to the biodiversity in the park occur when habitats are trampled or destroyed; when litter covers the ground; when the precious water that desert life relies on is used to fill water jugs or polluted with fecal coliform; when trails and roads blazed through fragile desert soils compact them so vegetation can't grow; when erosion occurs as a result; when the air is polluted with dust, automobile fumes, and campfire smoke; and when human beings place themselves above the delicate web of desert life.

Why preserve wilderness? Writer and environmentalist

Wallace Stegner wrote in his famous "Wilderness Letter": "Something will have gone out of us as a people if we ever let the remaining wild places be destroyed, if we permit the last virgin forests to be turned into comic books and plastic cigarette cases, if we drive the few remaining numbers of the wild species into zoos or to extinction; if we pollute the last clear air and dirty the last clean streams and push our paved roads through the last of the silence, so that never again will Americans be free in their own country from the noise, the exhausts, the stinks of human and automotive waste. And so that never again can we have the chance to see ourselves [as] . . . part of the environment of trees and rocks and soil, brother to the other animals, part of the natural world and competent to belong in it."

On a hot August morning, Michael, John, and I fill our water bottles and drive the loop road into the Ajo Mountains. Michael wants to photograph some of the unusual rock formations at Bull Pasture. Along the road, we stop to examine the ripe red fruits of the organ pipe cactus, which have split open to expose hundreds of tiny black seeds. They look like a colony of ants. Michael grabs a stick, pokes it into the fruit, and savors the bright red pulp. John and I do the same. It tastes sweet, like watermelon. The seeds make it crunchy.

At Bull Pasture trailhead, we put on our daypacks and hike up into the mountains. Jojoba and bluish-green agave grow out of solid volcanic rock, and the ocotillos are leafy green from a recent rain. It's getting hot, and although I've already drunk more than a quart of water, I begin to pant as we climb even higher. It's 104 degrees today, and I find myself stopping to catch my breath every few hundred yards. My face is crimson. My heart races. I feel nauseous and dizzy. I recognize these symptoms as the first stages of heat exhaustion, and at a switchback, I find a tiny patch of shade beneath a rock wall and sit there until my body cools down.

That's when the memories return, and I'm forced to recall the very first time I hiked up here alone and got miserably lost. I had wandered off the Bull Pasture Trail down into a canyon, then over a series of ridgelines. In a flat grassy area I was astounded to find a gathering of ancient sleeping circles and hearths used by the cultures that once passed through the park. In the arroyos below, I found tinajas full of water, some of them several feet deep. Light green algae floated on the surface like fishing nets. I felt very much like a time traveler as thin white clouds raced overhead, casting shadows over this ancient campsite.

In late afternoon that day, I climbed out of the canyon. Every ridgeline looked the same, and I retraced my steps over each of them at least three times, trying to find the Bull Pasture Trail. Only a few days ago, I had heard about a young woman, distraught by the breakup with her boyfriend, who'd hiked up here alone. She disappeared, some say near the Sphinx, though her body was never found. I was running out of water, becoming dehydrated. It was ninety-something degrees, but it would be cold that night in the mountains. I had no jacket. I had no food. I had no sleeping bag. At best, I could hike back to the sleeping circles and burn branches from the meager shrubs there to stay warm. I could drink water from the algae-filled tinajas. At worst, I could act rashly and try to make my way down the treacherous cliffs all around me that plummeted to the desert floor thousands of feet below. I gazed down and wondered what it would be like to be hurled like a stone through time and space and all the fleeting illusions of a lifetime. The desert stretched below me like the taut skin of a drum. I blinked and stepped back in a body I no longer seemed to occupy, then prayed aloud to whoever might be listening to get me down off the mountain before it grew dark.

Then, like something out of a dream, laughter echoed down the ridgeline to the east. It was a group of sunburned students from Prescott College who had spent the day on Mount Ajo learning how to contour—hike off-trail without a compass or a map. I thought they must be angels as they led me to the trail and back down the mountain in twilight.

Now, from my perch in the shade, I douse my head with water and follow John and Michael up the trail to Bull Pasture, where I sign the guest register at the top. A jackrabbit leaps through the brush, and in a canyon below, John spots a young deer drinking from a shallow pool where tadpoles struggle to survive as the water dries up. Dark clouds have built in the southeast, but the rain does not come.

On a nearby ridge, Michael notices something white lying on the ground. He stoops to pick it up, turning it over in his hand. "Looks like the foot of some kind of cat," he says. "A bobcat, maybe." It still has all of its claws.

"You want to see bones?" John calls from behind a boulder. "*Here's* some bones."

There in a pile lie a femur, some ribs, a hip bone, and a broken spine. The bobcat's skull is missing.

In a nearby clearing, I find the same ancient sleeping circles I stumbled upon the day I got lost. Flakes of chert lie on the ground next to an unfinished arrowhead made of quartz. Then we notice that one of the sleeping circles has been partially dismantled and that someone has recently used the rocks as a fire ring. Tiny pieces of charcoal litter the ground.

I keep looking back up at the ridgeline where the Bull Pasture Trail ends to establish a reference point. This time I don't want to get lost. John helps me orient myself, and I focus on two tall saguaros that rise against the skyline. We find the trail again without a hitch and hike back down the mountain in the blazing afternoon sun. I do not have the strength to revisit Seven Saguaro Camp on the other side of the park as I had wanted, not in August anyway. I will not know whether my old camp is safe, whether the saguaros have been spared the fate of knife-blade graffiti or other types of vandalism from the multitudes that pass through the park every single day. Some things should be left to mystery, I tell myself. I want to remember my desert sanctuary as it was: pristine and peaceful—a place of personal transformation that will forever be part of my deepest soul.

desert heart

W e come to the desert to understand things that are outside of ourselves, yet after a while, we are forced to look inside,
to find those precious sanctuaries that allow us to be truly alive
while truly alone. The greatest surprise of all, as I would find, is
that everything I need to know can be learned in the desert: joy,
sorrow, beauty, fear, trust, patience, tenacity. Here I can let go
of naming things and the constant need to know. In the desert,
knowledge comes intuitively if I listen. Time itself can be mea-
sured by the subtlest changes—the way the shadows fall across
the rocks, the position of the stars, the song of a white-winged
dove at dawn. Still, there are things I do not understand, mys-
teries I will never comprehend.

One afternoon while exploring the Cipriano Hills on the western edge of the park, I find an unexpected treasure: the sun-bleached skull of a coyote pup with all of its teeth intact. It's lying beneath a creosote bush, glinting in the sun. Gazing at the tiny head, I wonder what became of it. Perhaps a bobcat killed it, or a great horned owl swooped down and snatched the pup from its den while it slept, or maybe it died of disease. I wonder late into the night as a pack of its cousins yelp from a nearby arroyo as though they are calling down the moon.

At sunrise when I wake, I gaze into a mirror. I am tanned and thin, and my hair is two shades lighter. My eyes are clear, yet my heart is lonely. I feel an uneasy awareness, a transformation taking place as I shed my familiar sense of self like the skin of a very old snake. The paradox is that I am happiest alone in the desert, even though there have been times when what I wanted most was to share this place with another, to sit on a mountain long into the night, watching the stars spin the galaxy out like a giant web. "Some days we have to shoulder against a marauding melancholy," Gretel Ehrlich wrote in *The Solace of Open Spaces*. I know that others sometimes feel the same. It's part of the awkward transition between loneliness and solitude, the acceptance of what is.

It's morning and all the bajadas are full of water, as though they have become turquoise lakes floating between the mountains. I stand here alone marveling at this magical transformation of the desert when a man and a woman quietly appear beside me. They are dressed in animal skins, and they are placing brightly beaded bags along the

Ajo Mountains from Pinkley Peak foothills.

shoreline of the lake like some kind of offering. I ask them who they are. They tell me, but it's a culture I do not know, a language I do not understand. They give me one of the bags. It's made of deer hide and beaded with red and purple flowers. There is something inside, but I wake before ever knowing what.

Learning about the desert takes time. Edward Abbey once wrote, in *Slickrock,* that the best way to get to know it was to "Pick out a good spot and just sit there, not moving, for about a year. . . . Keep your eyeballs peeled and just sit there, through the hours, through the days, through the nights, through the seasons—the freeze of winter, the stunning glare and heat of summer, the grace and glory of the spring and fall—and watch what happens."

If solitude is a meditation on the world and tranquility transforms us, then Organ Pipe for me is the natural heartbeat of the desert. Here, the rhythm of the land beats slowly, and my imagination is forced to break through the barriers of space and time. Here it is possible to descend into the bare bones of my psyche and look as deeply into myself as any place on earth. And as if from a womb, there comes a feeling of merging with the wild earth like an embryo, a root, or a seed. Carl Jung once said: "Your vision will become clear only when you can look into your heart. . . . Who looks outside, dreams. Who looks inside, awakens."

I spend the day sitting quietly in the overhang of a shallow cave and later write this poem:

Becoming Nothing

Sitting here still as a mountain
mindful of dove-song and blossoms
I note hand, chest, head.
Body moves in ancient rhythms
rocking in some vast womb
like an imprint among stars.
Thigh, heart, eye become fluid
until there is no distinction.
I sit with heart full yet empty.
I sit for what the self is becoming
and for what it is not
until body rumbles like unstable earth
jarred by some unknown force.
Heart braces then shatters like ice,
leaving in this quaking breast
the birthplace of fire.

A long time passes before I return to the monument. My work takes me to South America, Africa, Asia, and the Pacific Northwest, but I know I will always come back. Here in this refuge, I have learned that the only certainty is change. On this miraculous planet we call home, we can leave something of our spirit behind and the desert will hold it, keep it safe among thorn and sun and stone. And when we return to the places that have forever changed us, we will know them, recognize them at once as our own, yet no one's — the invisible threads that connect us all.

about the author

Carol Ann Bassett is the author of *A Gathering of Stones: Journeys to the Edges of a Changing World* (Oregon State University Press), a finalist for the Oregon Book Award in Creative Nonfiction. Her essays have been anthologized in the American Nature Writing series and in *The Mountain Reader*, a Nature Conservancy book. Her work has appeared in *The New York Times, The Nation, Condé Nast Traveler*, in numerous other national publications, and on NPR. She lives in Eugene, Oregon, where she teaches magazine writing, environmental journalism, and literary nonfiction at the University of Oregon. Bassett lived in the Sonoran Desert for twenty-eight years.

about the photographer

Michael Hyatt has been photographing the people and the land-scapes of the American Southwest for more than thirty-five years. His work has illustrated numerous calendars, music collections, newspaper articles, postcards, and books, including *Beyond and Back: The Story of X; The Pleasures of Jazz: Leading Performers on Their Lives, Their Music, Their Contemporaries;* and *California Bloodlines.* Additionally, he has been exhibited in one-man and group photography shows in California, Colorado, Maryland, Washington, D.C., and Arizona. Michael's gallery representation is by Metroform Limited Photographic Art in Tucson, Arizona.

Library of Congress Cataloging-in-Publication Data

Bassett, Carol Ann.
Organ Pipe : life on the edge / text by Carol Ann Bassett ; photographs by
Michael Hyatt.
p. cm. — (Desert places)
ISBN 0-8156-2384-3 (pbk. : alk. paper)
1. Natural history—Arizona—Organ Pipe Cactus National Monument.
2. Organ Pipe Cactus National Monument (Ariz.) I. Hyatt, Michael, 1946–
II. Title. III. Series.
QH105.A65B37 2004
508.791'77—dc22
2004006900